THE WORK OF CHRISTMAS

The 12 Days of Christmas with Howard Thurman

THE WORK OF CHRISTMAS
The 12 Days of Christmas with Howard Thurman

Copyright © Bruce Epperly, 2017.

The publisher and the author wish to thank Friends United Press for their kind permission to use quotes from Howard Thurman's writing. We have changed the original text only to make it more gender inclusive, reflecting Thurman's inclusive and egalitarian vision of humankind.

Anamchara Books
Vestal, New York 13850
www.anamcharabooks.com

IngramSpark 2020 paperback ISBN: 978-1-62524-794-0

Scripture quotations are from the New Revised Standard Version Bible, copyright © 1989 National Council of the Churches of Christ in the United States of America. Used by permission. All rights reserved worldwide.

Illustrations by Jeffrey Thompson.
Design by Micaela Grace Sanna.

THE WORK OF CHRISTMAS

The 12 Days of Christmas with Howard Thurman

BRUCE G. EPPERLY

This text is dedicated to the beloved community at South Congregational Church, United Church of Christ, Centerville, Massachusetts, where we seek to learn, love, and live the word of God, and to three of my spiritual magi, who worked together for peace and reconciliation: Howard Thurman, Shorty Collins, and Allan Armstrong Hunter.

CONTENTS

Introduction:
A Word About Howard Thurman and the Twelve Days of Christmas   11

An Invitation to Adventure:
The Universality of Christmas   19

The First Day of Christmas:
The Character of God   25

The Second Day of Christmas:
The Joy of Christmas   31

The Third Day of Christmas:
The Beauty of the Season   35

The Fourth Day of Christmas:
The Promise of Christmas   39

The Fifth Day of Christmas:
The Angels of Christmas   43

The Sixth Day of Christmas:
The Dignity of Humankind   **49**

The Seventh Day of Christmas:
All Is Grace   **55**

The Eighth Day of Christmas:
Our Better Angels   **61**

The Ninth Day of Christmas:
Lighting the World   **67**

The Tenth Day of Christmas:
Christmas Amid Tragedy   **71**

The Eleventh Day of Christmas:
The Growing Edge   **77**

The Twelfth Day of Christmas:
The World of Christmas   **83**

The Road Ahead:
Epiphany Adventures   **89**

Sources   **93**

INTRODUCTION

A Word About Howard Thurman and the Twelve Days of Christmas

This book is a celebration of the twelve days of Christmas in dialog with the wisdom of one of my spiritual mentors, Howard Thurman (1899–1981). I wrote this book to deepen my experience of Christmas and as a way of making Christmas a lifelong adventure. My prayer is that you too will find yourself among the magi, shepherds, angelic hosts, farm animals, and the holy family as you read these words. Although intended for use during the Christmas season, Christmas, like Easter, is always a contemporary reality, which can be born in us with each new day. As the hymn proclaims, "Joy to the world, the Lord is come!"

I met Howard Thurman twice. First, at a lecture he gave at Grace Baptist Church in San Jose, California, in the early 1970s, when I was a long-haired college student at San Jose State University. His host was the Baptist College Chaplain George L. "Shorty" Collins, whom Thurman first met at a Fellowship of Reconciliation conference in the 1920s. Later, in 1976, when I was a doctoral student at Claremont Graduate University, I attended Thurman's lectures on spirituality at Scripps College in Claremont.

Born in Florida during the dark days of the Jim Crow era, Thurman rose to become the Dean of Rankin Chapel at Howard University and later the first African American to become Dean of the Marsh Chapel at Boston University. A civil rights activist, he also was co-founder of the Church of the Fellowship of All Peoples, in San Francisco, California, America's first intentionally interracial church. Thurman was the author of many books that have shaped my spiritual life, including *The Growing Edge; Deep River: Reflections on the Religious Insight of Certain of the Negro Spirituals; Deep Is the Hunger;* and *Jesus and the Disinherited*, one of the first texts in black liberation theology and a book that Martin Luther King often carried with him during the height of the Civil Rights struggle.

Thurman's spiritual perspective was shaped by two fundamental realities: his mystical experience of God's presence moving through all creation and giving dignity to all people and his experience as an African American, growing up under the oppression of "separate but equal" and "Jim Crow" laws. Thurman became aware of the limitations of his childhood faith, when the local church refused to conduct his father's funeral because he was an agnostic. When they finally found a minister to do the funeral, Thurman was appalled and angered when the preacher "preached his father into hell" in the funeral sermon. No longer able to experience God in the conservative Baptist tradition of his youth, he discovered God's gentle and healing presence in the rhythms of Nature. The woodlands and ocean reminded him that one great lung breathed through all creation, giving life and energy to all things and joining all things in a symphony of grace. Thurman believed that "all life, indeed all experience, is heavy with meaning, with particular significance."[1] Moreover, Thurman asserted that "there can be no thing that does not have within it the signature of God, the Creator of Life; the loving substance out of which all particular manifestations of life arise; there is no thing that does not have as part of its essence, the imprimatur of God, the Creator of all, the Bottomer of existence."[2] Along similar lines, the apostle Paul proclaimed to a multifaith crowd in Athens that God is the reality "in whom we live and move and have our being" (Acts 17:28).

Thurman's sense of God's presence in Nature and the depths of human spirit was a counterforce to the racism he experienced in pre–Civil Rights America and that many African Americans still experience in the United States today. One of the strongest influences on his understanding of God came from John Hope, President of Moorehouse College, where Thurman did his undergraduate studies. In speaking of Hope's impact, Thurman recalled:

> He always addressed us as "young gentlemen." What this term of respect meant to our faltering egos can only be understood against the backdrop of the South in the 1920s. We were black men in Atlanta during a period when the state of Georgia was known for its racial brutality. Lynchings, burnings, unspeakable cruelties were the fundamentals of existence for black people. Our physical lives were of little value. Any encounter with a white person was inherently dangerous and frequently fatal. Those of us who managed to remain

physically whole found our lives defined in less than human terms.[3]

By definition, racism denies or diminishes the presence of God in certain members of humanity, objectifying and excluding them from full membership in the human community as a result of the color of their skin and place in the social order. Only a deep sense of God's presence as our deepest reality can serve as an antidote to the brutal realities of racism and the traumatic impact of personal or institutional childhood abuse. The mystic vision inspires both self-affirmation—God is the deepest reality within which I live, move, and have my being, and I am God's child regardless of how others define me—and the affirmation that those who oppress me are also God's children and thus capable of spiritual transformation. This vision of human unity was a guiding force in Thurman's nonviolent political resistance to the evils of American racism and segregation and his novel attempts to bring the races together in synergetic encounters.

In speaking of the life experience that influenced his preaching, Thurman confessed that "inasmuch as my life is lived as a black man in a predominately white society, my personal adventures are profoundly influenced by this fact. The result is that in the most unlikely moment, there may spring into my mind an incident or experience that is mine because of this racial fact."[4] Through it all, Thurman sought what he referred to as the "growing edge"—"the extra breath from the exhausted lung, the one more thing to try when all else has failed, the upward reach of life when weariness closes in upon all endeavor"[5] —the spiritual movement toward healing and wholeness, which creates one human family despite the diversity of culture, race, and religion. In reflecting on his preaching ministry, Thurman asserted: "The core of my preaching has always concerned itself with the development of the inner resources needed for the creation of friendly world of friendly [persons]."[6]

This is the world we yearn for particularly at Christmas. During the twelve days of Christmas, our goal is to experience God's gentle providence despite the temptation to close our hearts in a world too often characterized by racism, sexism, polarization, nationalism, and exclusion. This is the work of Christmas, the growing edge that lures us toward God's realm of truth, beauty, and love.

My prayer for you is that the candles you light during the twelve days of Christmas will kindle your Christmas spirit throughout the entire year:

We light the candle of joy.
A candle to celebrate light in darkness,
Love that overcomes fear,
Joy that heals sorrow,
Faith that outlasts the machinations of power brokers and despots,
Hope that awakens us to new possibilities.
We light a candle of joy
For this present moment
When God is with us
And we share the light of God's love
Here and everywhere.
We light it with Mary and Elizabeth,
And Joseph, Jesus, and John the Baptist,
And light-bearers in all times and places,
As we open to God's love being born in us.

—Bruce Epperly

AN INVITATION TO ADVENTURE

The Universality of Christmas

*In the beginning was the Word,
and the Word was with God, and the Word was God....
All things came into being through this Word
and without the Divine Word not one thing came into being.
What has come into being
with the Word was life,
and the life was the
light of all people....
The true light, which enlightens
everyone,
was coming into
the world.*

John 1:1,3–4,9

When we build our crèche, light our special candles, decorate our evergreen with tinsel and color, hold our romantic tryst under the mistletoe, prepare the festive meal, share our gifts as the celebration of the privacy and universality of love, take the time to remember in many ways those who touched us in the midst of the traffic of the commonplace, and sing carols in honor of the birth [of Christ]—when we do these things we show that God has not been left without specific witness to Divine love and care of us who are God's children. To the strong and the weak, the happy and the sorrowful, to the barren and the fruitful womb, to the devout believer and the arrogant unbeliever, to the Christian and the non-Christian, there is the ever-present hope that tidings of great joy will find their way into the heart and life.

—Howard Thurman[7]

American poet Theodore Roethke asserts that in the darkness the eye begins to see. In the middle of a dark wood, when the path is uncertain, if we stand still long enough, our eyes adjust to the darkness and the contours of a pathway home appear. The story of Christmas is like that: it emerges out of the darkness—the darkness of Mary's womb, the darkness of bleak midwinter, the darkness of powerlessness and poverty, and the darkness of Roman occupation. In such a situation, it is difficult to believe that anything good can be born or that a child will survive the cruelty of despotic hatred. Yet, the story of this child's birth witnesses to light in the darkness and hope in a time of fear. The light of the world shines most brightly on the darkest night. In the moist darkness of the earth, a seed germinates, holding within itself the promise of a harvest to come.

The Gospel writers balanced the universal and the personal in their accounts of Jesus' birth. Born a Jew in first century Palestine, Jesus spent his whole life in an occupied land, powerless politically and with his back against the wall, as Howard Thurman notes in *Jesus and the Disinherited*. Our Savior's physical survival was totally at the mercy of the Romans and their Jewish minions, who could demand obedience arbitrarily and at any moment. Yet, in the humble stable, the everlasting light of God shines; "the hopes and fears of all the years" meet in Bethlehem on that long-ago birthday.[8]

Howard Thurman is a particularly appropriate interpreter of the message of hope that emerges out of darkness. Born in the South in 1899, Thurman, like the Christ Child, experienced the trauma of prejudice throughout his life. In his writing, he gives us several glimpses of what it meant to be a black man facing prejudice and discrimination. One autumn, young Howard worked a for a white store owner, raking leaves. After he raked the leaves into a pile, the store owner's four-year-old daughter decided to play a game. Whenever she saw a brightly colored leaf, she scattered the whole pile to show it to Howard. Although she meant no harm, she did this several times until Howard lost his patience and told her to stop. When she continued, he threatened to tell her father. Angered by his threat, the young girl jabbed him with a straight pen. When he cried out, the girl responded, "O Howard, that didn't hurt you. You can't feel."[9] Years later, now a successful church leader in Washington, DC, Thurman had to explain the spirit-destroying realities of "separate but equal" laws to his daughters when they wanted to play in a "whites-only" playground during a visit to relatives in Florida.

In contrast to the illusions of the rich and famous, who deny privilege based on birth, race, and economics, God comes to us at Christmas among the poor and forgotten. Those who have had their backs against the wall due to economic and racial discrimination—African Americans pulled over without cause by law enforcement officers and legal citizens treated as if they are "illegal aliens"—can understand the radical message of Christmas better than those who live in penthouses and gated communities. Without privilege, they, like the impoverished shepherds who first heard the angelic alleluias, know that the powers and principalities can crush them at any moment. After Christ's birth, the Holy Family had to flee to Egypt to save their beloved child from the machinations of the religious and political leaders. Refugees in a strange land, like many of today's undocumented workers, political refugees, and their children, Jesus and his family survived because of the kindness of strangers who accepted them despite their immigrant status.

Emmanuel, God with us, is the message of Christmas in the darkness of our own times, when our nation is polarized and people fear the future. God is with the Muslim family bullied on their way home from a mosque, a gay couple whose right to marry is challenged by "good Christian" folks, a child left behind during recess because of his learning disability, an elder abandoned by relatives in a nursing facility, and unemployed Central Pennsylvania machinists who blame their plight on immigrants and persons of color rather than the greed of American corporations. In the apparent darkness of our times, we need to remember that God is still with us as we pray:

> *O holy Child of Bethlehem*
> *Descend to us, we pray*

Cast out our sin and enter in
Be born to us today.
We hear the Christmas angels
The great glad tidings tell
O come to us, abide with us
Our Lord Emmanuel. [10]

A Christmas Practice

Take a few minutes each day to be still in God's presence. Let the words of "O Little Town of Bethlehem" be your prayer. Ask God to be born in you and give you faith for the living of our times.

A Christmas Prayer

O Holy Child of Bethlehem, be born in us today. Cast out our sin, and enter in. Fill us with your light amid the darkness of our time. Let us be lights in our world, living witnesses that love is stronger than fear, that Christ is alive in our lives and the world. In Christ's name. Amen.

THE FIRST DAY OF CHRISTMAS
(DECEMBER 25)

The Character of God

The Father and I are one. . . .
If I am not doing the works of my Father,
then do not believe me. But if I do them,
even though you do not believe me,
believe the works, so that you may know

> *and understand that the Father is in me*
> *and I am in the Father.*
> John 10:30,38

> *If God is and [God] is love, as I believe most profoundly and if in Jesus there is the projection of this central affirmation in concrete flesh and blood, then in such a person there are inevitably precious clues as to the meaning of God and the meaning of Life. His way of life, then, becomes the way of life at its highest and best.*
> —Howard Thurman [11]

Our faith tells us that if we want to know God's true character, we need to look at Jesus and his ministry. On Christmas morning, we discover that the heart of the Incarnation is not about theological doctrines, moral guidance, commandments, or dramatic revelations; but the birth of a baby, an ordinary event that has occurred several billion times, which, in its simplicity, reveals God's relationship with humankind and the nonhuman world. The Word and Wisdom of God, the creative artistry of the universe, and the energy of the Big Bang—all take flesh in the vulnerability and innocence of a newborn baby.

Take a moment to reflect on the birth of Jesus or the birth of the children in your life. At first they simply sleep, cry, eat, and poop. They are completely vulnerable, helpless, needy, and totally dependent on the loving care of others. Their lives depend on the Grace of Interdependence, the intricate connectedness that gives birth to compassionate care and sustaining love. Grace is everything—a love not earned but deserved and given—to the little ones in our midst.

Nothing is more ordinary yet amazing than the birth of a child. Nothing can be more complicated and subject to fate than a child's birth. When our son and grandchildren were born, they received all the benefits of a middle-class, privileged American birth—good health care, a nursery waiting for them, and parents who could imagine their lives as unfolding in terms of good schools, college, and successful and creative adulthoods. This isn't the case for many children today, nor was it the case for Mary and Joseph's baby. Jesus was the child of working-class parents, who were economically insecure and politically powerless. Jesus' parents were in Bethlehem for his birth because they had no choice. They would have preferred for Jesus to have been born in their home town, Nazareth, but Caesar Augustus demanded that they—and thousands of other families—travel to the village of Joseph's family line to register for taxation. Mary and Joseph would have far rather had the comfort of their own home for the birth of their first child. Instead, they were not only far from home, but there was also no place for them to stay. Like other homeless families, they had to settle for whatever they could find—a spare room, a stable, a cave, or even the open air—for the birth of Jesus.

As I write these words, with Christmas carols playing in the background, I feel a deep spiritual disturbance as whole families are being massacred in Aleppo for no other reason than they happened to be in the wrong place at the wrong time. God have mercy on us! Forgive us, we know not what we are doing as we helplessly look on their martyrdom, while frightened and hard-hearted politicians and church leaders speak out against welcoming refugees to the United States.

Thirty years ago, American singer-songwriter Joan Osborne asked, "What if God was one of us?" and then described the experiences of fallible and forgotten people, simply trying to find their way home. In the Bethlehem stable, we discover that Emmanuel, "God with us," is best understood not as an all-powerful and distant Caesar, immune from human misery, but as fully connected with human life or, as the philosopher Alfred North Whitehead says, "the fellow sufferer who understands." A few years after Whitehead's affirmation of God's intimacy with us, Dietrich Bonhoeffer, protesting the inhumanity of the Nazi regime from a prison in Germany, asserted that "only a suffering God can save."

The Christmas stories show us God with us, fully immersed in the messiness of daily life, in experiences of vulnerability and powerlessness, at the mercy of heartless and uncaring political leaders. The Incarnation brings heaven to earth, and it brings earth to heaven. A stable—and our own homes—become chock-full with divinity, and God becomes fully aware of the sorrows and joys of human life. God is part of the intricate interdependence of life, feeling the full range of hope and fear, touched by a child's cry as bombs rain down in Aleppo or the grief of the parent of a teen shot down in the city streets of America.

God rejoiced when you were born and delighted in your moments of achievement and spiritual transformation. God's power is love, not coercion, exclusion, or violence. God changes the world by living in our midst and inviting us to care for the lost, lonely, and forgotten, for that is where we will find this little Child. As another Christmas hymn proclaims:

Jesus is our childhood's pattern,
Day by day, like us he grew,
He was little, weak and helpless,
Tears and smiles, like us he knew;
And he feels for all our sadness,
And he shares in all our gladness.[12]

A Christmas Practice

As you read the newspaper, watch the news, or go about your errands, look for Jesus in the faces of those with whom you interact. Look for God in weakness as well as wonder—for the great wonder is that God is with us in all the ordinariness and struggle of daily life and that Jesus is born in a slum and not a penthouse.

A Christmas Prayer

Open our eyes to the wonder of your presence in our joy and pain. Let us see your birth and nurture your Child in us and those we meet. In the name of the Christ Child. Amen.

THE SECOND DAY OF CHRISTMAS

(DECEMBER 26)

The Joy of Christmas

*But the angel said to them,
"Do not be afraid, for see—
I am bringing you good news of
great joy for all people:
to you is born this day in the city of David,
a Savior who is the Messiah, the Lord.*

Luke 2:11

The mood of Christmas—what is it? It is the quickening of the presence of other human beings into whose lives a precious part of our own has been released. It is the memory of other days in which an angel appeared spreading a halo over an ordinary moment or a commonplace event. It is an iridescence of sheer delight that bathes one's whole being something more wonderful than words can ever tell.

—Howard Thurman [13]

Christmas is about delight and wonder. It is about experiencing the joy of family and friends, about becoming large-spirited persons, willing to let go of grievances, forgive and forget, and let love guide our way. It is about the sparkle in a child's eyes, when she sees presents under the tree and the ecstasy of a young boy bouncing a new basketball or racing around the house with his Star Wars *Millennium Falcon*.

The spirit of Christmas creates a mood in which commonplace events become portals into divinity, and everyday encounters place us on holy ground. "Do you hear what I hear?" queries a carol. If we train our ears, there is a song in the air—a baby's cry, a shepherd's laugh, a wise man's affirmation—and it is the song of God within and around us.

"In the bleak midwinter," God's glory shines. On the shortest days, when the sun sets in midafternoon, a light guides our way. We see this light in the faces of children and discover this holy light in our own hearts. Every moment reveals eternity and we are joined with loved ones everywhere, in this world and the next.

If we open our hearts to the Christmas spirit, we will discover life as too wonderful to imagine. There will be no words, simply gratitude for the opportunity to share in Jesus' birth and experience this little child in every encounter.

> *Joy to the earth! The Savior reigns,*
> *Let all their songs employ;*
> *While fields and floods, rocks hills and plains,*
> *Repeat the sounding joy, repeat, repeat the sounding joy.* [14]

A Christmas Practice

Take time today to pause and look for the light in those around you. See the light of God in a companion napping in front of the television, the boundless energy of a young child, the faces of politicians enamored of publicity rather than service, faces of all colors and persons of all economic strata. If you encounter a homeless or vulnerable person, look for the light within that individual and ask God what you might do to ease the pain of the lost, lonely, and forgotten of your town and nation. Choose joy for yourself and those you meet.

A Christmas Prayer

Loving God, help us to see your light and follow your star wherever it takes us. Give us vision to see your presence in the forgotten and lonely and give us your wisdom to respond with grace and love. In Jesus' name. Amen.

THE THIRD DAY OF CHRISTMAS
(DECEMBER 27)

Beauty of the Season

The wilderness and the dry land shall be glad,
the desert shall rejoice and blossom;
like the crocus it shall blossom abundantly,
and rejoice with joy and singing.
Isaiah 35:1–2

> *The quality of Christmas—what is it? It is the fullness with which fruit ripens, blossoms unfold into flowers, and live coals glow in the darkness. It is the richness of vibrant colors—the calm purple of grapes, the exciting redness of tomatoes, the shimmering light on the noiseless stirring of a lake or a sunset. It is the sense of plateau with a large rock behind which one may take temporary respite from the winds that chill.*
>
> —Howard Thurman[15]

John's Gospel proclaims that Jesus' mission has the goal that we might have life and have it abundantly (John 10:10)—and Christmas is about life in its fullness. It is about celebrating beauty in a world where brutality and oppression are everyday experiences for millions of persons, including our most vulnerable children. In the Christmas season, we rejoice in the warmth of a fire, bright poinsettias, holly and ivy, and colorful lights on the tree. During Christmas, our senses are trained to look for beauty.

We may not have words for what we experience, but we realize that there is more to life than we previously imagined. Angels hide in every nook and cranny, magi masquerade as everyday people, and shepherds wear the garments of day laborers. The whole earth is brimming with glory for those with eyes to see and ears to hear. As the philosopher Alfred North Whitehead asserts, the aim of the universe is toward the production of beauty, whether in the swirling galaxies, redwood trees and placid ponds, geese flying overhead, or the wrinkles on a grandparent's face. Beauty is the gift of contrast, diversity, novelty, and transformation.

"Taste and see that God is good," chants the psalmist, and we can experience God in the world of flesh just as God experiences us in the manger at Bethlehem (Psalm 34:8). Rejoice! God is here, God is with us, born as a humble child, and growing in our lives. Dazzled by beauty where we least expect it, we are inspired to praise and witness:

> *Down in a lowly manger, the humble Christ was born,*
> *And God sent us salvation that blessed Christmas morn.*
> *Go tell it on the mountain, over the hills and everywhere,*
> *Go tell it on the mountain that Jesus Christ is born.* [16]

A Christmas Practice

Give thanks for the beauty of this world and make a commitment to bring forth beauty wherever you find yourself, whether by a kind word, a simpler lifestyle, a commitment to care for the Earth, or a random act of kindness. The world is saved one act at a time.

A Christmas Prayer

Help us to live by joy, to taste and see beauty, and to bring forth beauty in every encounter. Help us to love this good Earth. Remind us that prophets and not profits show us and our nation the way to following you. In Christ's name. Amen.

THE FOURTH DAY OF CHRISTMAS

(DECEMBER 28)

The Promise of Christmas

Then the eyes of the blind shall be opened,
and the ears of the deaf unstopped;
then the lame shall leap like a deer,
and the tongue of the speechless sing for joy.
For waters shall break forth in the wilderness,
and streams in the desert.
Isaiah 35:5–6

The symbol of Christmas—what is it? It is the rainbow arched over the roof of the sky when clouds are heavy and foreboding. It is the cry of life in the newborn babe, when forced from its mother's nest, it claims the right to life. It is the brooding presence of the Eternal Spirit making crooked ways straight, rough places smooth, tired hearts refreshed, dead hopes stir with newness of life. It is the promise of tomorrow at the close of every day, the movement of life in defiance of death, and the assurance that love is sturdier than hate, that right is more confident than wrong, that good is more permanent than evil.

—Howard Thurman[17]

Christmas is the promise of tomorrow, embodied in the adventures of today. The Prince of Peace is born among us and invites us on a holy adventure in which we discover that love is stronger than fear, reconciliation more powerful than hate, and peace more enduring than violence. Christmas asks us and our leaders to live by a new standard and to choose a new way of life.

Christmas looks forward. Incarnate in a manger over two thousand years ago, God is also the voice of tomorrow, the moral arc of history calling us forward to horizons of hope and affirmation. God is fully here and now—but God's realm lies in the future, inviting us to be citizens of a world not yet born.

The politics of Christmas is guided by love, not coercion; understanding, not name calling; embracing, not bullying; solidarity, not division; and sacrifice, not greed. On

Christmas, no child is forgotten, no adult is left behind, and the wealthy and powerful discover that sacrifice, not hoarding, is the path to the Christ Child.

We who have been to the graveside know the pain of loss—the loss of a dear friend, a child, a parent, a spouse. At Christmas, we remember our pain and vow to combat all needless death that comes through violence, neglect, or greed. In affirming "the movement of life in defiance of death," we discover Eternity in the midst of time, we are joined with loved ones whom we mourn, and we gain the vision of Life Everlasting and the joyous reunion with God and our loved ones in which Love Endures Forever. With the carolers, we sing:

How silently, how silently, the wondrous gift is given.
So God imparts to human hearts the blessings of his heaven.
No ear may hear his coming, but in this world of sin,
Where meek souls will receive him still the dear Christ enters in.[18]

A Christmas Practice

As you read the morning paper, skim the Internet for the latest stories, or listen to the news on tele-

vision or the radio, let the information you receive touch your heart and inspire your hands. What one thing can you do, based on what you've seen, to make the world more beautiful and loving? What one act of generosity can you perform to warm a weary soul or strengthen another's hope? Your response can be as simple as calling a friend who mourns the loss of a loved one . . . writing a check to an organization that supports vulnerable children or endangered species . . . asking your congressional representative or senator to respond to opioid addiction or advocate environmental protection . . . or reaching out to someone with whom you've had a grievance.

A Christmas Prayer

God of light and love, awaken us to the amazing wonder of today and our chance to spread your good news to the world. Help us become your peacemakers and healers in a world of violence and pain. In Jesus' name. Amen.

THE FIFTH DAY OF CHRISTMAS

(DECEMBER 29)

The Angels of Christmas

In that region there were shepherds living in the fields, keeping watch over their flock by night. Then an angel of the Lord stood before them, and the glory of the Lord shone around them, and they were terrified. But the angel said to them, "Do not be afraid; for see—I am bringing you good news of great joy for all the people."
Luke 2:8–10

> *There must be always remaining in every[one]'s life some place for the singing of the angels—someplace for that which in itself is breathlessly beautiful and by an inherent prerogative throwing all the rest of life into a new and created relatedness. Something that gathers up into itself all the freshets of experience from drab and commonplace areas of living and glows in one bright light of penetrating beauty and meaning—and then passes. The commonplace is shot through now with new glory—old burdens become lighter, deep and ancient wounds lose much of their old, old hurting. A crown is placed over our heads that for the rest of our lives we are trying to grow tall enough to wear. Despite all the crassness of life, despite all the harshness of life, life is saved by the singing of angels.*
>
> —Howard Thurman[19]

In the first century, shepherds lived a rough and tumble life. At the lower end of the social spectrum, living from paycheck to paycheck, with no security for their old age, if they made it that far, we would describe them today as the working poor. More than that, because of their rough ways and lack of etiquette, they were viewed as shiftless, the sort of folk you wouldn't leave alone with your wallet or purse. But, like many of today's working poor, who are neglected and scorned by Wall Street, erudite intellectuals, and big-business politicians, they still had dreams. They hoped for a better world for themselves and their families. They dreamed of escaping the cycle of poverty. They quietly longed for a political revolution, a messianic leader, who would defeat the Roman legions and make Israel great again. They were skeptical of the religious leaders and the big-city politicians, especially those who promised greatness and gave the spoils of power to cronies who had a vested interest in the growing gap between the poor and the rich.

And yet, on a dreary, wintry night, the shepherds heard the "First Noel." As the song says, "to certain poor shepherds on fields where they lay on a cold winter's night that was so deep." They were astounded that angels would come to people like them, and not to kings and millionaires. But the Christmas story announces that God has a particular love for the poor. Powerless, the poor know that they need a Rescuer. They have no riches to insulate them from the deep awareness that they need help, simply to get by, stay on the right path, and find some small portion of meaning in lives neglected by the powerful and secure.

Howard Thurman notes that one of the greatest tragedies of poverty and powerlessness is a constricted imagination that stifles our ability to dream big for ourselves or our children. In ghetto neighborhoods and Appalachian communities, many parents simply hope for their children to make it to adulthood. Children's hopes are stunted by gun violence, parents addicted to drugs, and images of gangs as the source of community. For those without defense or power, God is their only hope!

The wealthy and powerful may also have stunted imaginations. Often, they define the good life in terms of consumerism and power over others, prioritizing profits over compassion. They may value the monetary gain of lower taxes more than they do the beloved community, where all God's children in every land can live toward a vision of creativity and beauty.

All of us need the aspiration that comes from an angelic encounter. In Thurman's words, we need a crown "placed over our heads that for the rest of our lives we are trying to grow tall enough to wear." Angels come into our lives, bringing tidings of great joy, opening our eyes to beauty, giving us second chances, and filling ordinary days with wonder. Pause a moment, listen for the singing of the angels. With the shepherds, listen for the voice of the future calling you to holy adventures.

Silent night, holy night,
Shepherds quake at the sight,
Glories stream from heaven afar,
Heavenly hosts sing alleluia;
Christ the Savior is born! Christ the Savior is born! [20]

A Christmas Practice

Who are the "shepherds" in our community? Who do we pass by without noticing? Be attentive to the "shepherds"—the store clerk working at minimum wage, the stock person at the big-box store, the person or family receiving government aid and school lunches. While we may not be able to influence directly the economics of these modern-day shepherds, we can recognize their need for housing, higher wages, and dignity. If we too belong to these groups, we can remember we are God's beloved children and we can claim justice in the marketplace and in the political arena.

A Christmas Prayer

God of dreams and visions, give us a broken and contrite heart for those who live in poverty, for the working poor, the homeless family, the opioid addict, the forgotten and lost. Let us remember that as we do unto the least of these, we do unto you, O God. In Christ's name. Amen.

THE SIXTH DAY OF CHRISTMAS

(DECEMBER 30)

The Dignity of Humankind

You are the light of the world;
a city build on a hill cannot be hid. . . .
Let your light shine before others,
so that they may see your good works
and give glory to your Father in heaven.

Matthew 5:14,16

> *Jesus remains the symbol of the dignity and worthfulness of the common humankind. . . . If the theme of the angels' song is to find fulfillment in the world, it will be through the common person's becoming aware of her or his own worthfulness and asserting her or his generic prerogatives as a child of God.*
>
> —Howard Thurman[21]

"You are worthy. You are my beloved children." That is the message of Christmas.

While some misguided theologians and preachers say that God loves us in spite of whom we are, Christmas proclaims that God loves us just as we are, because we are God's beloved children. The angelic announcement to the shepherds and Christ's birth in a rough-hewn manger, a feeding trough for farm animals, proclaims God's identification with humanity in all its imperfection and wonder. "For God so loved the world that he sent his only begotten son" (John 3:16). God is born in human life to save and heal, not condemn. God comes to love and not punish. God is not out to get us. God is out to love us.

"You are the light of the world and God's light shines in and through you." God's message to us is that regardless of who you are or where you are on life's journey, you belong.

You matter. You are loved, and nothing can separate you from the love of God. God looks upon you with the same love that Mary and Joseph looked upon Jesus, and the love with which new parents look on their own newborn child. God is misty eyed with love for you, and God is doing and will do everything in God's power to show you how wonderful you are and help you discover the gifts that bring joy to you and the world around you.

The challenge of the "common person" is to recognize and claim her or his worth. The Advent and Christmas scriptures spotlight two women, Elizabeth and Mary, unlikely bearers of divine revelation. Elizabeth is described as "barren" in a world in which women were judged by their fertility. Mary is too young and inexperienced—and frankly too unimportant—to be the "mother of God." Like billions of women, then and now, Mary and Elizabeth were pushed to the sidelines and valued primarily for their roles in a patriarchal social order. Yet, the Nativity places Mary and Elizabeth at the center of divine revelation along with outsider shepherds and foreign magi.

The Christmas story places each of us at the center of God's love. We are essential to God's Shalom (the peaceful, healthy, fulfilled way of life that is God's vision embodied on earth as it is in heaven). Worthy of love, we love others. Worthy of gifts, we encourage the gifts of others. Forgiven of our imperfection and sin, we forgive others. Accepted, we accept others, especially the forgotten, scorned, and hated. We are God's companions in healing the world, one act at a time. In the stories of Christmas and the Christ Child, we see what we can be as companions in God's realm.

And our eyes at last shall see him, through his own redeeming love;
  For that child so dear and gentle is our Lord in heaven above,
    And he leads his children to the place where has gone.[22]

A Christmas Practice

Throughout the day, say silently or quietly, "I am God's beloved child," "I am God's beloved son," or "I am God's beloved daughter." Let that phrase also be in your heart as you encounter others on your path: "You are God's beloved child," as you treat them with respect and dignity.

A Christmas Prayer

Loving Creator, remind me of your great love for me. Let me love myself, and out of that love, give me a heart of love for all your children. Let me know my worth as your beloved child, blessing others as I have been blessed. In Christ's name. Amen.

THE SEVENTH DAY OF CHRISTMAS (DECEMBER 31)

All Is Grace

When the angels had left them and gone into heaven, the shepherds said to one another, "Let us go now to Bethlehem and see this thing that has taken place, which the Lord has made known to us." So they went with haste and found Mary and Joseph, and the child lying in the manger. When they saw this, they made known what had been told them about this child; and all who heard it were amazed at what the shepherds told them. But Mary treasured all these words and pondered them in her heart. The shepherds returned, glorifying and praising God for all they had heard and seen, as it had been told them.

Luke 2:15–20

> *The story of Christmas has certain very simple human things in it which appeal to my kind of mind and spirit. A family—a man, a woman, and a child—animals, simple surroundings, the primary family unit. There is always the possibility that the first steps in love, in confidence, in trust can be measured, developed, expanded. So when we think of Christmas, let us think of it as a time when we remembered the graces of life. It is important to seize upon the atmosphere created in this period, to let it tutor our own spirits in kindness and imaginative sympathy. Thus we may be able to give ourselves freely to the babies in our midst, to sustain them into their growth in youth and maturity. We must do our part to guarantee that all children may have the chance to be children, to experience their own childhood. . . . There can be no good future for [humankind] if this sensitivity to the birth and meaning of the child that we see in Christmas is ignored.*
>
> —Howard Thurman [23]

The old year is ending and soon we will have a chance to begin again, to dream of becoming new persons; to let go of bad habits, begin new and healthy behaviors, and resolve to live with greater mindfulness and compassion. As we look back on the bygone year, let us release past burdens and painful memories. Let us forgive the sins of others and let go of grievances. Let us begin as new persons for a new year, open to new possibilities, gracefully bestowed upon us by the hand of God.

Christmas is a time for children and the child in us. It touches our heart because it celebrates the birth of a child. Yet the spirit of Christmas remains dormant until we bless the child within—seeking healing from the trauma of our own childhood—and bless the children around us by our attention, compassion, and active support. When we hear a child wailing, our first response should be to ask, "Why is that child crying?" –and then, "How can we ease her or his pain?" This is also true of the adult child in us and others. We all need God's healing touch to transform childhood wounds into windows of grace.

Howard Thurman was well aware of the suffering some children experience. Poverty, racism, and war rob children of their childhoods. These tragic realities stifle the imagination, as children and their parents simply try to survive, amid falling bombs, gunshots in the streets, unemployment, and hatred because of race, ethnicity, sexuality, or religion.

In the language of South African spirituality, *Ubuntu*—"I am because of you"—is at the heart of the Christmas message. None of us can find true fulfillment until every child has a home, a healthy diet, adequate health care, safe schools, and the laughter of loving homes and supportive communities. At Christmas, let us protect the innocence of each child, so that, in Thurman's words, "all children have the chance to be children, to experience their childhood."

> *Away in a manger, no crib for his bed,*
> *The little Lord Jesus lay down his sweet head;*
> *The stars in the sky looked down where he lay,*
> *The little Lord Jesus asleep on the hay. . . .*
> *Be near me, Lord Jesus, I ask thee to stay*
> *Close by me forever, and love me I pray.*
> *Bless all the dear children in thy tender care,*
> *And fit us for heaven, to live with thee there.*[24]

A Christmas Practice

Take note of the children in your midst. In what ways can you affirm their gifts and support the innocence of childhood? Take note of children in pain and poverty. In what ways can you affirm their lives, support their innocence, and advocate for a social order where every child matters and no child—or family—is left behind?

A Christmas Prayer

O Little Child of Bethlehem, descend on us we pray, cast out our sin and enter in, be born in us today. Help us midwife the well-being of the children in our midst. Help us to pay attention and respond with love. Melt our hardheartedness that we may love without measure, sacrificing from our plenty that all children might have joy. In the name of the Christ Child, Jesus our Savior. Amen.

THE EIGHTH DAY OF CHRISTMAS
(NEW YEAR'S DAY)

Our Better Angels

Now the birth of Jesus the Messiah took place in this way. When his mother Mary had been engaged to Joseph, but before they lived together, she was found to be with child from the Holy Spirit. Her husband Joseph, being a righteous man and unwilling to expose her

to public disgrace, planned to dismiss her quietly. But just when he had resolved to do this, an angel of the Lord appeared to him in a dream and said, "Joseph, son of David, do not be afraid to take Mary as your wife, for the child conceived in her is from the Holy Spirit. She will bear a son, and you are to name him Jesus, for he will save his people from their sins." All this took place to fulfill what had been spoken by the Lord through the prophet: "Look, the virgin shall conceive and bear a son, and they shall name him Emmanuel," which means, "God is with us." When Joseph awoke from sleep, he did as the angel of the Lord commanded him; he took her as his wife, but had no marital relations with her until she had borne a son; and he named him Jesus.

Matthew 1:18–25

The true meaning of Christmas is expressed in the sharing of one's graces in a world in which it is so easy to become callous, insensitive, and hard. Once this spirit becomes part of a [person]'s life, every day is Christmas and every night is freighted with the dawning of fresh, and perhaps holy, adventure.

—Howard Thurman[25]

Christmas calls us to follow our highest and best visions of ourselves in our daily lives, occupations and avocations, and citizenship. It asks that we set aside selfishness and reach out, past our differences, offering love, forgiveness, and healing to every situation we encounter.

In a time of deep national turmoil, that greatest of American presidents, Abraham Lincoln counseled in his inaugural speech: "We are not enemies, but friends. We must not be enemies. Though passion may have strained, it must not break our bonds of affection. The mystic chords of memory will swell when again touched, as surely they will be, by the better angels of our nature." Years later, after the South had been defeated and the slaves emancipated, Lincoln was asked how he would treat the Confederacy now that the war was ending. His inquisitor expected words of vengeance, appropriate to the blood shed by Northern soldiers and the evil wrought upon the nation, but Lincoln replied, "I will treat them as if they never left." He responded with grace rather than anger, forgiveness rather than hatred.

Joseph's circumstances were very different from Lincoln's, but Joseph also faced a challenge to which he could have responded with the "normal," expected reaction—or with grace. After he learned that Mary was pregnant, he wanted to do the right thing, but he was uncertain what course of action would be best. We don't know how he responded to her explanation that this unplanned pregnancy came from the hand of God. How would you take it if the woman you loved became pregnant and you were not the father? How would you respond to a mystical explanation for your partner's pregnancy? In Joseph's case, he was uncertain about maintaining his engagement with Mary. No doubt he weighed the cost of breaking off his engagement and leaving Mary to face her pregnancy alone, given the patriarchal realities of the time. He wasn't sure that he could be the father, but he did not want to disgrace Mary or put her life at risk. My suspicion is that he prayed for guidance. From his fervent prayers emerged an answer in the form of a dream.

Dreams often convey a deeper wisdom than does everyday consciousness. God speaks to us a variety of ways, including through the unconscious, intuitions, hunches, and synchronous encounters. Joseph dreamed of angelic visitation, revealing the true nature of Mary's child. Touched by an angel, Joseph stayed by Mary's side, supporting her during the pregnancy, accepting his role as Jesus' father.

Joseph shows us the incarnation of graceful relatedness. He lives with his uncertainty, trusting God's wisdom and gracefully honoring his relationship with Mary, regardless of the baby's origins. Like Elizabeth and Mary, Joseph's response is grace in action.

Thurman reminds us that "the true meaning of Christmas is expressed in the sharing of one's graces in a world in which it is so easy to become callous, insensitive, and hard." With the birth of a new year, we can make a commitment to live as if "every day is Christmas." We can embrace the coming of a new year as an invitation to holy adventure. God wants us to be large-souled people, living by grace and giving by grace, as we let the joy of Christmas guide us the whole year long.

Let us follow Joseph's example and make grace our personal and political goal in the year ahead. We will cherish what we don't fully understand, recognizing with Joseph that the reality of God and others is not always understandable—but it is embraceable.

This gift of God we'll cherish well,
That ever joy our hearts will fill.
How great our joy! Great our joy!
Joy, joy, joy! Joy, joy, joy!
Praise we the Lord in heaven on high!
Praise we the Lord in heaven on high! [26]

A Christmas Practice

Today, give and receive grace. Pause to see the pain and aspiration of those around you. Awaken to your own innocence and God's love for you. Let go of guilt and shame, and let go of grudges in the personal, corporate, and political realms. We may advocate for certain political policies—as Christ's followers, our calling is to "let justice roll down like waters, and righteousness like an ever-flowing stream" (Amos 5:24)—but when we challenge inequality and the heartlessness of political leaders, let us do so with love and not fear or hate.

A Christmas Prayer

Holy God, let me in the New Year give your grace to those near to me and share grace in my relationships. Let me be your companion in healing, one act at a time, bringing joy and light to the darkness and love to the lost in our midst, whether they are powerful or weak, wealthy or poor. In Christ's Name. Amen.

THE NINTH DAY OF CHRISTMAS

(JANUARY 2)

Lighting the World

*The light shines in the darkness
and the darkness did not overcome it.*

John 1:5

*I will light Candles this Christmas;
Candles of joy despite all sadness,
Candles of hope where
despair keeps watch,
Candles of courage
for fears
ever present,
Candles of
peace for tem-
pest-tossed days,*

Candles of grace to ease heavy burdens,
Candles of love to inspire all my living,
Candles that will burn all the year long.
　—Howard Thurman[27]

Christmas is not merely a single day or twelve days. It is a way of life.

Christmas begins in darkness—the darkness of the womb, the darkness of human violence and oppression, the darkness of hopelessness, the darkness of wayward humankind. In Christmas, we recognize that a light shines, and that the darkness can never defeat it. We recognize that God's light streams into the most unexpected places—a stable, among foreign magi from another religious tradition (likely from Persia, today's Iran), and in the varieties of human culture and ethnicity. As John's Gospel proclaims, God's light and wisdom, God's word, creates all things. "The true light, which enlightens everyone, was coming into the world" (John 1:9). Just a little light can transform the darkness and help the anxious pilgrim find her or his way.

Howard Thurman tells the story of being caught in a summer thunderstorm. He had gone berry picking and plunged in the woods behind his grandmother's house, wandering far off the familiar path. Caught up in the joy of plucking ripe berries from the bushes, Thurman was startled into awareness by a flash of lightning, followed by a crash of thunder. As the sky darkened, Thurman felt completely lost and panic set in. On the verge of running just to do something, he remembered something his grandmother had told him: when you don't know where you are, stop and look around until you see something familiar. So young Howard stopped still and waited, training his eyes on the landscape with each lightning strike, until he saw something familiar. From then on, each lightning strike illuminated his path until he found his way home.

With chaos all around, we too can discover a quiet center in the storm and, like Howard Thurman, find our way home. And as we find our way, we can also help others on their pilgrimages. Our lives can enlighten the world.

Jesus describes us as "the light of the world," whose calling is to "shine" so that others might come to experience God (Matthew 5:14–16). Each day, we can light candles of joy, hope, courage, peace, and love, committing ourselves to bringing life and light to the world.

Silent night! Holy Night! Son of God, love's pure light.
Radiant beams from thy holy face,
With the dawn of redeeming grace,
Jesus, Lord, at thy birth, Jesus, Lord, at thy birth.[28]

A Christmas Practice

Each day as the New Year begins, you can light a candle—or candles—to maintain the Christmas spirit. In the spirit of votive candles, you may have a particular intention: safety for our troops, protection of the environment, the well-being of every child, homes for the homeless, your own healing, the well-being of a loved one, or the mission of your church. Commit yourself to be a light in the world in all that you do.

A Christmas Prayer

As I light a candle today, let me be a light bearer. Let me be an instrument of your peace and a light unto the world. In Christ's Name. Amen.

THE TENTH DAY OF CHRISTMAS
(JANUARY 3)

Christmas Amid Tragedy

In the sixth month the angel Gabriel was sent by God to a town in Galilee called Nazareth, to a virgin engaged to a man whose name was Joseph, of the house of David. The virgin's name was Mary. And he came to her and said, "Greetings, favored one! The Lord is with you." But she was much perplexed by his words and pondered what sort of greeting this might be. The angel said to her, "Do not be afraid, Mary, for you have found favor with God. And now, you will conceive in your womb and bear a son, and you will name him Jesus."

Luke 1:26–31

Where refugees seek deliverance that never comes,
And the heart consumes itself, if it would live,
Where little children age before their time,
And life wears down the edges of mind,
Where the old person sits with mind grown cold,
While bones and sinew, blood and cell, go slowly down to death,
Where fear companions each day's life,
And Perfect Love seems long delayed.
CHRISTMAS IS WAITING TO BE BORN:
In you, in me, in all humankind.
   —Howard Thurman[29]

Christmas is an ambiguous and tragically short-lived season. After the packages have been unwrapped and the dishes washed, we often return to business as usual. We forget that in God's realm, Christmas is the norm—the natural state of affairs—and that our consumerism, apathy, neglect of the vulnerable, and greed-inspired economics are the exceptions.

Christmas comes to those with their backs against the wall, as Thurman asserts: working-poor shepherds, a family having to migrate to satisfy a dictator's need for riches despite a mother's pregnancy, infants murdered by a local ruler in his quest to destroy the Holy Child and his way of peace. And as we celebrate the twelve days of Christmas, we too witness wars and rumors of war. Swords are not beaten into plowshares but fashioned into drones, automatic weapons, and missiles. Nations continue to study war and encroach on their neighbors' territories. Whole communities are annihilated, often inspired by religious ideology that separates faithful from infidel and "saved" from "unsaved."

As a pastor, I see the personal tragedies as well: the loneliness of nursing home residents, the diminished imaginations of children whose parents are among the unemployed or working poor, the pain of traumatized adults, the anguish of those singled out because of race or sexuality, the grief of families at the death of a child or the loss of a parent or spouse through Alzheimer's. You've seen similar situations, I know. In the face of so much pain, our hearts break, and we are tempted to become hopeless and heartless ourselves.

Yet, in such moments of despair, the quiet providence of God whispers that life can be different. Christmases past and present don't determine, as Ebenezer Scrooge discovered, the Christmases to come. Regardless of the morality of our leaders, we can be citizens of a world in which Shalom-

Peace reigns supreme and a little child shall lead us. We can raise the bar of our own spirituality and ethics to embrace humankind and the nonhuman world and live as if Love is the only sustaining reality.

We may need to be wise—and savvy—in fulfilling our role as citizens. Yet a politics of love always trumps a politics of fear and hate. At the end of the day, no one remembers Herod or Caesar Tiberius, and we barely remember Pilate (the rulers whose quest for power and control led to Jesus' crucifixion), but that Little Child lives on forever. He inspires our imaginations, guides our footsteps, and challenges us and our leaders when we place consumption and greed about planetary well-being and self-interest above care for the vulnerable.

The birth of the Little Child of Bethlehem tells us that we can be born again. The healer from Bethlehem inspires us to have large and expansive spirits and hearts, inviting us to experience each day as a holy adventure, with God as our companion and all creation as brothers and sisters. And in the dark days, when it seems that evil will triumph, we can resonate with Henry Wadsworth Longfellow's poem "Christmas Bells," written when his son was wounded during a Civil War battle:

I heard the bells on Christmas Day
Their old, familiar carols play, and wild and sweet
The words repeat of peace on earth, good-will to men!
And thought how, as the day had come,
The belfries of all Christendom had rolled
along the unbroken song
Of peace on earth, good-will to men!
Till ringing, singing on its way,
The world revolved from night to day
A voice, a chime, A chant sublime
Of peace on earth, good-will to men!
Then from each black, accursed mouth
The cannon thundered in the South,
And with the sound the carols drowned
Of peace on earth, good-will to men!
It was as if an earthquake rent
The hearth-stones of a continent,
And made forlorn the households born
Of peace on earth, good-will to men!
And in despair I bowed my head;
"There is no peace on earth," I said;
"For hate is strong, and mocks the song
Of peace on earth, good-will to men!"

Then pealed the bells more loud and deep:
"God is not dead, nor doth He sleep,
The Wrong shall fail, the Right prevail,
With peace on earth, good-will to men." [30]

A Christmas Practice

Be aware of places and occasions where you can respond to loneliness, pain, and vulnerability. Reach out to a child or a resident of a nursing home. Give your heart as well as your treasure to bring joy to the world.

A Christmas Prayer

Loving Companion, help us to see your face and hear your voice in the refugee, the forgotten senior adult, the lonely child, the anxious parent. Help us to give our hearts and hands to bring beauty to their lives. In Christ's Name. Amen.

THE ELEVENTH DAY OF CHRISTMAS

(JANUARY 4)

The Growing Edge

And now, you will conceive in your womb and bear a son, and you will name him Jesus. He will be great, and will be called the Son of the Most High, and the Lord God will give to him the throne of his ancestor David. He will reign over the house of Jacob forever, and of his

kingdom there will be no end." Mary said to the angel, "How can this be, since I am a virgin?" The angel said to her, "The Holy Spirit will come upon you, and the power of the Most High will overshadow you; therefore the child to be born will be holy; he will be called Son of God. And now, your relative Elizabeth in her old age has also conceived a son; and this is the sixth month for her who was said to be barren. For nothing will be impossible with God." Then Mary said, "Here am I, the servant of the Lord; let it be with me according to your word." Then the angel departed from her.

Luke 1:31–38

Look well to the growing edge! All around us worlds are dying and new worlds are being born; All around us life is dying and life is being born. The fruit ripens on the tree; the roots are silently at work in the darkness of the earth against a time when there shall be new leaves, fresh blossoms, green fruit. Such is the growing edge! It is the extra breath from the exhausted lung, the one more thing to try when all else has failed, the upward reach of life when weariness closes in upon all endeavor. This is the basis of hope in moments of despair, the incentive to carry on when times are out of joint and [people] have lost their reason, the source of confidence when worlds crash and dreams whiten into ash. The birth of the child—life's most dramatic answer to death—this is the growing edge incarnate. Look well to the growing edge!

—Howard Thurman[31]

God says, "Behold, I do a new thing."

The new thing that God seeks often occurs in times of disruption, when the familiar world has collapsed and the future is in doubt, when the days grow shorter, and we wonder if darkness will swallow the light. The new thing that is being born in our lives emerges out of the hidden womb and the dark soil. God's new thing is the vision of "something more," a hovering possibility that challenges the world as it is. It is the moral arc toward which history bends, filling us with a divine restlessness with the way things are that inspires the quest for what may be if the world embraces God's vision of Shalom.

Robert Kennedy once asserted, "There are those that look at things the way they are, and ask why? I dream of things that never were, and ask why not?" Another martyr to the violence that has plagued our nation, Martin Luther King (building on the wisdom of Theodore Parker) asserted:

Evil may so shape events that Caesar will occupy a palace and Christ a cross, but that same Christ arose and split history into A.D. and B.C., so that even the life of Caesar must be dated by his name. Yes, "the arc of the moral universe is long, but it bends toward justice." [32]

Christmas is the impossible dream of what could be and is not yet achieved. It is the dream of the lion and the lamb as playmates, of swords beaten into gardening tools, of the wealthy sacrificing for the poor, and the powerful initiating policies for the well-being of today's children and children unborn to the seventh generation. Without this dream, without impossibilities that challenge our weary realism, we would be content with a world of violence, hate, prejudice, and poverty. Without this dream, bullying, racist comments, and hate crimes would be seen as normal and not violations of what is best in humankind. Without this dream, infidelity would be the norm and faithfulness an aberration.

But God has a dream—the dream of Shalom—emerging when we least expect it and the powers of darkness appear to be winning. God's dream inspires our dreams for a new earth, mirroring a new heaven. In the words of Martin Luther King, whose vision of America reflected Thurman's:

I have a dream that my four little children will one day live in a nation where they will not be judged by the color of their skin but by the content of their character. . . . I have a dream that one day every valley shall be exalted, and every hill and mountain shall be made low, the rough places will be made plain, and the crooked places will be made straight; and the glory of the Lord shall be revealed and all flesh shall see it together.[33]

A baby changes everything. A baby is an image of hope that life can be more beautiful and that we can be more loving and that even in the humblest environment, angels sing. For us this season, this baby is Jesus, and he is constantly being born in our lives, blessing us to bless the world.

Christmas is about tomorrow as well as today. It is about God's dream becoming our dream and God's child becoming our child. Look well to the growing edge!

> *What can I give him, poor as I am?*
> *If I were a shepherd, I would bring a lamb;*
> *If I were a wise man, I would do my part;*
> *Yet what I can, I give him; I give him my heart.*[34]

A Christmas Practice

What impossibility can you imagine for your life, your community, and the world? What is your hope for the future—your own, your community's, and the world's? In what ways can you take the first steps in achieving your hope, in making it come alive in the world today and tomorrow? Make a commitment to be part of God's growing edge.

A Christmas Prayer

Help us be ambassadors and midwives of the growing edge. Help us plant seeds for tomorrow and dream of a better world. Bless our imaginations and give us energy to make God's dream come true in our lives and the world. In Christ's name. Amen.

THE TWELFTH DAY OF CHRISTMAS

(JANUARY 5)

The Work of Christmas

In the time of King Herod, after Jesus was born in Bethlehem of Judea, wise men from the East came to Jerusalem, asking, "Where is the child who has been born king of the Jews? For we observed his star at its rising, and have come to pay him homage." When King Herod heard this, he was frightened, and all Jerusalem with him; and calling together all the chief priests and scribes of the people, he inquired of them where the Messiah was to be born. They told him, "In Bethlehem of Judea; for so it has been written by the

prophet: 'And you, Bethlehem, in the land of Judah, are by no means least among the rulers of Judah; for from you shall come a ruler who is to shepherd my people Israel.'"

Then Herod secretly called for the wise men and learned from them the exact time when the star had appeared. Then he sent them to Bethlehem, saying, "Go and search diligently for the child; and when you have found him, bring me word so that I may also go and pay him homage." When they had heard the king, they set out; and there, ahead of them, went the star that they had seen at its rising, until it stopped over the place where the child was. When they saw that the star had stopped, they were overwhelmed with joy. On entering the house, they saw the child with Mary his mother; and they knelt down and paid him homage. Then, opening their treasure chests, they offered him gifts of gold, frankincense, and myrrh.

Luke 2:1–11

When the song of the angels is stilled,
When the star in the sky is gone,
When the kings and princes are home,
When the shepherds are back with their flock,
The work of Christmas begins:
To find the lost,
To heal the broken,

To feed the hungry,
To release the prisoner,
To rebuild the nations,
To bring peace among brothers [and sisters],
To make music in the heart.
   —Howard Thurman [35]

King Herod was frightened of a little baby! Imagine that! A world based on fear—whether of refugee children, like Jesus and his family, or today's political refugees—will eventually collapse from its isolation and hard-heartedness. Love always trumps fear and hate. Love opens us to novelty and wonder, and inspires us to bring beauty to daily life, to the lives of the vulnerable, and to the world. Yes, joy and beauty to the world, because God is here!

Christmas is a season, but it is also a state of mind that dwells tenderly on the simple things, that looks for beauty in ugliness, and seeks peace in conflict. On this twelfth day of Christmas, we don't need partridges, rings, or maids a milking; we need the dream of God's realm to energize and challenge us. Let us make a commitment to become Christmas people, builders of a new world, embracing persons in need and seeing Christ born and reborn in every child. Let us pray to take our Christmas spirit into the season of Epiphany, the season of the Persian magi and God's revelation in unexpected places.

The light of the world still shines. It shines in me and you and all creation, and the darkness can't extinguish it. Let us be God's revelation—shining like stars in the heavens—to give light to every weary pilgrim. Let us go forth in God's light.

Break forth, O beauteous heavenly light, and usher in the morning;
O shepherds, shudder not in fright, but hear the angels warning.
This child, now weak in infancy, our confidence and joy shall be,
The power of Evil breaking, our peace eternal making.[36]

A Christmas Practice

Throughout the day and in the weeks ahead, pause a few moments for quiet prayer and meditation and take time to read Thurman's poem. Let it guide your thoughts and your paths. Commit yourself to be a Christmas person all year long.

A Christmas Prayer

There are times, God, when we feel powerless and unimportant. We let the powerful and wealthy determine our values and our future. Show us the value and purpose of our own lives, and the role we have in saving the world. Let us live by the vision of your Shalom: to find the lost, to heal the broken, to feed the hungry, to release the prisoner, to rebuild the nations, to bring peace among brothers and sisters, to make music in the heart. In Christ's name. Amen.

THE ROAD AHEAD

Epiphany Adventures

And having been warned in a dream not to return to Herod,
they left for their own country by another road.
Matthew 2:12

Once this spirit becomes part of a [person]'s life, every day is
Christmas and every night is freighted with the dawning of fresh,
and perhaps holy, adventure.
   —Howard Thurman [37]

From the East, the magi came following a star. Spiritual leaders from another faith tradition—likely the light-spirited religion of Zoroaster—they experienced God's light in the far country of the Jewish people. They found the baby in a humble home far from the powerful and educated of Jerusalem, and they worshipped the Child of Israel, who was to become the Savior of all people.

The Feast of Epiphany proclaims God's revelation in unexpected places and among unexpected people. The true light enlightens everyone—Buddhists, Hindus, Muslims, Jews, and agnostics—as well as followers of Jesus. We find this light everywhere.

Inspired by a dream, the magi "left for their own country by another road." We never know where a dream can take us. The light can take us to unexpected places. Holy adventures can't be predicted, but one thing is certain: noticed or unnoticed, obvious or hidden, God will guide us as we go forth, following stars and dreams toward unexpected destinations. And in the midst of the journey, we may discover with feminist theologian Nelle Morton that "the journey is home"—that right now, God's grace is enough, beauty reigns supreme, and we have enough love and wisdom to find our way.

We take down the tree, we pack up the stockings, and store the cards till next year. But, the work of Christmas has just begun. God is with us!

The adventure continues!

SOURCES

[1] Howard Thurman, *With Head and Heart: The Autobiography of Howard Thurman* (New York: Harcourt Brace and Company, 1979), 268.

[2] Ibid., 269.

[3] Ibid., 36.

[4] Ibid., 161.

[5] Howard Thurman, *The Growing Edge* (Richmond, IN: Friends United Press, 2014), 17.

[6] Ibid., 160.

[7] Howard Thurman, *The Mood of Christmas & Other Celebrations* (Richmond, IN: Friends United Press, 1985), xi-xii.

[8] Phillips Brooks, "O Little Town of Bethlehem," 1868.

[9] Howard Thurman, *With Head and Heart* (New York, NY: Harcourt Brace and Company, 1979), 12.

[10] Phillips Brooks, "O Little Town of Bethlehem," 1868.

[11] Howard Thurman, *The Mood of Christmas & Other Celebrations* (Richmond, IN: Friends United Press, 1985), 8.

[12] Carl F. Alexander, "Once in Royal David's City," 1848.

[13] Howard Thurman, *The Mood of Christmas & Other Celebrations* (Richmond, IN: Friends United Press, 1985), 3.

[14] Isaac Watts, "Joy to the World," 1719.

[15] Howard Thurman, *The Mood of Christmas & Other Celebrations* (Richmond, IN: Friends United Press, 1985), 3.

[16] John W. Work, "Go Tell It on the Mountain," 1909 (based on an African American spiritual).

[17] Howard Thurman, *The Mood of Christmas & Other Celebrations* (Richmond, IN: Friends United Press, 1985), 3.

[18] Phillips Brooks, "O Little Town of Bethlehem," 1868.

[19] Howard Thurman, *The Mood of Christmas & Other Celebrations* (Richmond, IN: Friends United Press, 1985), 10.

[20] Joseph Mohr, "Silent Night! Holy Night!," 1818.

[21] Howard Thurman, *The Mood of Christmas & Other Celebrations* (Richmond, IN: Friends United Press, 1985), 11.

[22] Cecil F. Alexander, "Once in Royal David's City," 1848.

[23] Howard Thurman, *The Mood of Christmas & Other Celebrations* (Richmond, IN: Friends United Press, 1985), 12.

[24] John Thomas McFarland (v.3), Anonymous (v.2), "Away in a Manger," late 19th century.

[25] Howard Thurman, *The Mood of Christmas & Other Celebrations* (Richmond, IN: Friends United Press, 1985), 19.

[26] Nach Friedrich von Spee, "While by My Sheep," translation of a German carol, 1625.

[27] Howard Thurman, *The Mood of Christmas & Other Celebrations* (Richmond, IN: Friends United Press, 1985), 19.

[28] Joseph Mohr, "Silent Night! Holy Night!," 1818.

[29] Howard Thurman, *The Mood of Christmas & Other Celebrations* (Richmond, IN: Friends United Press, 1985), 21.

[30] Henry Wadsworth Longfellow, "Christmas Bells," 1863.

[31] Howard Thurman, *The Mood of Christmas & Other Celebrations* (Richmond, IN: Friends United Press, 1985), 23.

[32] Martin Luther King Jr., "Out of the Long Night," *The Gospel Messenger* (General Brotherhood Board, Elgin, IL: 8 February 1958).

[33] ———, "I Have a Dream," (speech, Lincoln Memorial, Washington, DC: 28 August 1963).

[34] Christina Rossetti, "In the Bleak Midwinter," *Scribner's Weekly*, 1872.

[35] Howard Thurman, *The Mood of Christmas & Other Celebrations* (Richmond, IN: Friends United Press, 1985), 23.

[36] Johann Rist, "Break Forth, O Beauteous Heavenly Light," 1641 (trans. by John Troutbeck).

[37] Howard Thurman, *The Mood of Christmas & Other Celebrations* (Richmond, IN: Friends United Press, 1985), 19.

BECOMING FIRE!
SPIRITUAL PRACTICES FOR GLOBAL CHRISTIANS

In the spirit of God's call to creative transformation, Bruce Epperly invites you to join him on a holy adventure in spiritual growth, inspired by the evolving wisdom of Christianity and the world's great spiritual traditions, innovative global spiritual practices, and emerging visions of reality. Epperly explores the many resources of Christian spirituality in dialogue with the spiritual practices of the world's great wisdom traditions, describing the gifts other spiritual paths contribute to the pathway of Jesus; at the same time, he uses the lens of the spiritual practices Jesus has inspired throughout Christian history to examine these spiritual paths.

Paperback Price: $24.95
Paperback ISBN: 978-1-62524-455-0

Kindle Price: $8.99
Kindle ISBN: 978-1-62524-456-7

SANTA CLAUS
Saint, Shaman, & Symbol

If you don't believe in Santa, you might want to reconsider. The familiar fellow dressed in red has been around a lot longer than the malls' Santa, longer than Rudolph, longer even than "The Night Before Christmas." His earliest and most ancient forms brought hope and cheer to generation after generation of humankind—and he still has a message for us today. In the midst of the materialism of the modern holiday, Santa offers us a bridge between the physical, secular world and the spiritual, sacred realm. Discover his history and evolution, from Ice Age shaman to medieval saint to modern-day icon. Get to know Santa—and believe all over again.

Paperback Price: $12.95
Paperback ISBN: 978-1-62524-464-2

Kindle Price: $5.99
Kindle ISBN: 978-1-937211-85-1

AnamcharaBooks.com

www.ingramcontent.com/pod-product-compliance
Lightning Source LLC
Chambersburg PA
CBHW060536080526
44586CB00012B/758